Russian Travel Made Easier: *Advice for Friends*

by Elena Istomina and Natalia Khrystolubova
Illustrator Sergey Dulin

WARNING AND DISCLAIMER:

Every effort was made to ensure that the information was correct at the time the book went to press. Nevertheless, to make an informed decision, you are advised to verify the information prior to purchasing any third party products or services described in the book. Any web sites linked to or from this book or products or services listed herein are not affiliated in any manner with the authors or Trafford Publishing House.

Neither authors of the book nor Trafford publishing shall have any liability arising from your purchases of third party products or services based upon the information provided in the book.

Order this book online at www.trafford.com/07-2717
or email orders@trafford.com

Most Trafford titles are also available at major online book retailers.

Note for Librarians: A cataloguing record for this book is available from Library and Archives Canada at www.collectionscanada.ca/amicus/index-e.html

ISBN: 978-1-4251-6000-5

www.trafford.com

North America & International
toll-free: 1 888 232 4444 (USA & Canada)
phone: 250 383 6864 • fax: 250 383 6804 • email: info@trafford.com

The United Kingdom & Europe
phone: +44 (0)1865 722 113 • local rate: 0845 230 9601
facsimile: +44 (0)1865 722 868 • email: info.uk@trafford.com

10 9 8 7 6 5 4 3 2

Contents

OUR TEAM

Elena Istomina was born and raised in Moscow. In 1994 she moved to the United States and found her second home in the Florida Keys. Elena is Director of International Programs at Seacamp where young people from all over the world discover the wonders of marine biology. When visiting Moscow twice a year she lectures at several universities including Moscow State Pedagogical University, where she received her PhD and taught English grammar for twenty years. Dr. Elena Istomina is the author of several textbooks which are presently being used in the English Departments of several Russian Universities.

Natalia (Natasha) Khrystolubova was born and raised in Siberia. In 1990 she moved to the United States. She lives and works as a pharmacist in Fort Myers, Florida. Natasha is an experienced and independent traveler who has mastered the art of online booking. She uses the Internet to book transportation, accommodations, tours, and all activities. Her expertise contributes greatly to this book.

Sergey Dulin is from Belarus. He graduated from graphic design school in Mogilev in 2007 and continues his successful artistic career with Fantasy World, Inc., an intellectual board game developer and distributor in Moscow.

We consider our friends a part of the team. We are grateful for their support, encouragement, and input through the process of working on the book.

Our thanks to Victoria, Heather, Irene, Kathy, Cheryl, Carol, Leigh, Ray, and Sally. Special thanks go to Max Istomin for his contribution to the book project.

So Russia is on your mind...

Then you have the right book in your hands.

You have probably been looking at hundreds of travel guides and survival kits trying to decide which book to buy. It is not an easy choice. Most of the books contain precious information on history, geography, culture, and major sights of interest. So why is this travel book special?

It is special because it was written by Russians who have lived in America for the past decade. During our frequent visits home, many of our American friends came along and we helped them to discover Russia as we know it. Through word of mouth the news spread quickly. People were calling with questions and looking for helpful hints on how to travel to Russia. Upon their return, many of them called back to share their stories. They described their experiences, both good and bad. We realized that what comes naturally to a native Russian could be a hindrance for tourists. These personal accounts helped us understand the visitor's perspective of Russia. They also opened our eyes to the kind of advice that would be the most valuable.

We have both been answering questions about Russian travel for the past twenty-five years. This gave us an idea of writing a book of friendly advice for visitors, regardless of the length of their stay. It is also a handy reference book providing a list of useful websites and travel books with concise and easy-to-read chapters on Russian history, culture, traditions and customs.

Our goal was to help travelers become Russia savvy and to help make their trip to Russia an unforgettably joyful experience.

CHAPTER 1

Getting Ready: Entry Visa and Money Issues

Traveling to Russia, whether it's for business or pleasure, requires a visa. A Visa is a permit to enter a country.

There are two ways of getting a visa:

• You can use the full visa processing service offered by some travel agencies. It is possible to complete the procedure through their websites or by phone. It is an easier but more expensive way to get a visa. Based on the prices and the quality of the customer service, we recommend the following websites: **www.waytorussia.net; www.gotorussia.com; and www.russia-travel.com.**

If the full visa processing service suits your needs, go ahead and fill out the application forms, attach the required documents including two recent passport-size photos. Enclose your passport and send the package to the address provided on the website. Sit back and relax. It will take 10-15 days to get the visa. The standard processing fee is from $150.00 to $200.00. The above-mentioned companies also offer express service at $250.00 - $300.00. Business visas are more expensive.

• You can do it yourself through the Russian Embassy and its Consulate services. First you need to obtain an invitation. You can do that by going to **www.russianconsulate.info.** Click on the type of visa you need, then on "*Apply for Russian Visa Invitation and Voucher*". After you get the visa support document you can download visa applications from the Russian Embassy website and apply for a visa through their consulate service. For more information check the Russian Embassy website **www.russianembassy.org.**

When in Russia, you need to register within the first three business days. Hotels have a standard registration procedure. However, if you are renting an apartment or staying with friends, it is the responsibility of the landlord or the inviting party to register you. You may choose to go to the nearest post office, and for a modest fee of approximately 180 rubles (slightly over $7.00), fill in the registration form and mail it. You will need a copy of your passport and a migration card issued at the passport control upon arrival in Russia. To read more about visa registration go to TalkLounge at **www.waytorussia.net**.

MONEY ISSUES

The Russian customs regulation allows to bring in up to $3,000.00 in undeclared cash. You may be better off with banknotes of different denominations, new and crisp. If you have damaged, worn-out, heavily stained, or torn bills, Russian banks may charge an extra fee for exchanging them.

The amounts in traveler's checks are not restricted, however, traveler's checks are not the most economical way to travel in Russia. Some merchants do not cash them; others that do, may charge an additional fee. It would cost you less in ATM fees when you withdraw funds from your debit or credit card. Find out from your bank what your daily limit is on cash withdrawals. Ask the bank to raise the limit if you plan to use your credit card extensively.

Foreign transaction surcharge rates may vary from 1% to 3% and it would be useful to know which credit card is less expensive to use. It might also be a good idea to ask your bank how much they charge on foreign transactions. It is important to notify the bank of your destinations so that the bank does not cancel your card on a suspicion of fraudulent use while you are overseas. For detailed information check **www.FlyerGuide.com** under the section "*Credit Cards Foreign Exchange Fees*".

Shopping centers, hotels and other tourist places accept all major credit cards, including American Express, Visa, and MasterCard. However, we have to admit that Visa is the most universal card and has the largest global electronic payments network.

A small calculator is handy for calculating a fluctuating exchange rate.

CHAPTER 2

Language Hints: Metro or Underground?

FAMILIARIZE YOURSELF WITH BRITISH ENGLISH

In Europe and Russia students are taught the British version of the English language. Sometimes the British and American synonyms can become a source of misunderstanding. The word "restroom" is a good example.

Several years ago, when one of our American friends arrived in Moscow and passed through customs, a guide from the travel agency met him. He asked the guide if he could stop at the restroom before heading to the city. To his utter surprise the guide informed him that the airport did not have any restrooms. Well, thought our friend, I was warned that Russia was full of surprises, but not having a restroom in a major international airport is a little too much. While he was preparing to tough it out a little longer, he suddenly realized that the guide, in an attempt to comfort him, mentioned that the drive to the city was quite short and the hotel had a comfortable room for him to rest. The word 'rest' rang a bell and it dawned on him that the guide was talking about a room to rest and not about a restroom. To his great relief the Sheremetievo International Airport had more than one facility called toilet.

To avoid confusion, here is an example of a few synonyms of American and British English. Remember that the British version is going to be the most familiar to English speaking Russians.

American version	***British version***
Apartment	*Flat*
Appetizer	*Starter*
Area code	*Dialing code*
ATM	*Cash machine*
Autumn	*Fall*
Billion	*Milliard*
Bun	*Roll*
Candy	*Sweet*
Call	*Ring*
Downtown	*Town center*
Eggplant	*Aubergine*
Elevator	*Lift*
Floor lamp	*Standard lamp*
Garbage/trash	*Rubbish*
Garbage can	*Dustbin*
Gas	*Petrol*
Ground floor	*First floor*
Intersection	*Cross road*
Last name	*Surname*
License plate	*Number plate*
Liquor	*Spirits*
Lobby	*Foyer*
Main street	*High street*
Underground	*Metro*
Movie	*Film*
Oatmeal	*Porridge*
Orchestra seats	*Stalls*
Pitcher	*Jug*
Railroad	*Railway*
Rent	*Hire (about cars)*

Restroom	*Toilet, WC*
Round trip ticket	*Return ticket*
Scallion	*Spring onion*
Shrimp	*Prawn*
Sneakers	*Trainers*
Store	*Shop*
Streetcar (in American English it is any form of public transport not powered by combustion engine).	*Tram or trolley bus (a British word tram is used for vehicles that run on steel rails and trolley bus for rubber tired vehicles that are powered by electricity taken from overhead conductors).*
Trash can	*Dust bin*
Trunk	*Boot (of a car)*
Vacation	*Holiday*
Wallet	*Purse*
Windshield	*Windscreen*

LEARN A BIT OF RUSSIAN BEFORE YOU GO

Now that you've thought about differences between American and British English, let's move on to Russian. Armed with a few essential phrases and simple practical questions, you will definitely feel more confident when you arrive in Russia. (Note: reading signs requires the knowledge of the Cyrillic alphabet). Being able to ask for directions to the nearest subway station, a restaurant, a taxi stand, or to the closest restroom can be a relief. No matter how hard you try to learn a foreign language in a couple of months, it is just impossible. Of course you could always carry a phrase book, but as a Russian joke goes, "there's nothing as useless as a good old phrase book." You might find the much-needed question, but will you understand the answer?

Here are some recommendations for software and Russian textbooks.

- ***Russian in 10 minutes a Day*** by Kristine K. Kershul, Kamal Bouranov, Marianna Ilyina, Alla A. Smyslova. Amazon offers it at $13.57 new, and used starting at $2.50
- ***Rosetta Stone*** is one of the most popular, dynamic and interactive soft-

ware language programs. You can watch its demo and buy it on line at **www.rosettastone.com** They offer the First level of Russian for $209.00, the Second level for $239.00 or a set of level 1&2 at $339.00

- ***Linkword© language courses*** were developed by Michael Gruneberg, a famous memory expert. Using a special memory technique, the course allows you to learn up to a 100 words an hour. They offer the Silver series (levels 1&2) at $69.99. Read more about the course at **www.unforgettablelanguages.com.**

There are several free Internet sites that offer Russian lessons:

- **www.listen2russian.com** (good audio sound)
- **www.byki.com**
- **www.russianlessons.net**
- **www.russnet.org/home.php**

Note: This site is maintained by the American Council of the Teachers of Russian. It offers interesting information both on Russia and places to learn the language while you are there.

- **www.guidetorussia.org/culture/russian-language**
- **www.skypetutoring.com/russian_lessons.html**

Note: This site offers live lessons given by Russian tutors via Skype.

CHAPTER 3

Flying Options: Welcome Aboard

If you haven't purchased a package that includes the plane ticket, you will have to buy the ticket yourself. Some Internet sites offer interesting deals. Here are a few sites where you can compare prices.

- **www.travelfleamarket.com**

- **www.kayak.com**
- **www.expedia.com**
- **www.cheaptickets.com**
- **www.travelocity.com**
- **www.lowfare.com**
- **www.orbitz.com**
- **www.planetickets.com**
- **www.bt-store.com**
- **www.flyaow.com**

Do not hesitate to book Aeroflot if it offers the best price. Aeroflot has undergone a complete makeover in the past decade and now its service meets the international standards. Besides, in 2006 Aeroflot joined the SkyTeam Airline Alliance, along with Delta, Continental Airlines, Northwest Airlines, Aero Mexico, Air France, Dutch Airlines and others. Aeroflot and Delta share the Moscow route, which means that people buying tickets through Delta or Aeroflot may be on the same plane flying to Russia.

Direct flights to Moscow originate in two East Coast cities: from New York (9 ½ hours) and from Atlanta (10 ½ hours). Direct flights from Atlanta to Moscow are served by Delta. Aeroflot flies directly to Moscow from Los Angeles on the West Coast, in approximately 13 hours.

You may opt for quick connecting flights with major European air carriers. For example, Lufthansa flies to Moscow via Frankfurt, Air France via Paris, British Airways stops in London, KLM makes a stopover in Amsterdam, while Alitalia stops in either Milan or Rome. If flying time is important go for a direct flight, but remember, the quickest route is usually the most expensive. If you are on a tight budget, book a connecting flight; it is cheaper than a direct flight.

Remember to take into consideration the time difference and add an extra day to your travel. In other words, if you leave the U.S. on the 5th of March you'll arrive on the 6th. When flying back to the U.S. you'll gain time. So if you leave Moscow on the 5th of March you'll arrive in the U.S. on the same day.

Low season prices are unbeatable. In January 2007 Aeroflot offered flights from New York to Moscow for $616.00. High season prices are usually increased to $1,500.00 on a similar joint Delta/Aeroflot flight.

Low Season is usually between the second week of January and the 1st of April, and from September until the first week of December. Shoulder Season begins in April and lasts until the 1st of June. Peak season is between June 1st and August 31st, and between December and the first week of January. You can often find good bargains on Easter, Christmas, or Thanksgiving Day when many Americans stay home with family and friends. Fridays and Saturdays are usually the most expensive departure days, while Saturdays and Sundays are the most expensive days for the return.

Moscow has two international airports: Sheremetievo (SVO) and Domodedovo (DME). Only British Airways flies from the U.S. to Domodedovo, a private airport offering the same facilities found in the world's best airports. Although there are no porters, the airport provides free luggage carts and assistance is available for passengers traveling with children under 3 years old. A local train connects Domodedovo Airport to downtown Moscow and to the Metro system. It is the most economical way to get to the city, but travel light as you will encounter many stairs along the way. For more details about transportation to and from the airports go to **www.wikitravel.org** and type *Moscow* in the search window.

If your plans include traveling within Russia, domestic tickets can be bought on the two websites we mentioned above: **www.waytorussia.net** and **www.gotorussia.com** or at **www.visitrussia.com.** You can also call East Line Air and Travel at 212-207-3081. The East Line Group is a Domodedovo managing company with an office in both New York and Moscow. They offer compatible domestic prices and their service is excellent.

We would also recommend using a travel agency; they can usually find the best flight at the best price in only a few minutes. That doesn't mean that you shouldn't do your homework and check what is available on the Net before contacting the agent or agency that specializes in travel to Russia. Here are some of them:

- Go to Russia:
  1-888-263-0023
- Russia House:
  1-877-600-7272
- Russian-American Corporation:
  1-877-268- 2677

❋ East West Tours:
1-800-776-3341

❋ Vega Travel:
1-800-359-8437

❋ Encore Travel:
1-800-787-7422

❋ Cinderella Travel Corporation:
1-877-275-8434

❋ Panorama Travel:
1-800-204-7130

❋ White Pearl Travel:
1-866-999-0599

❋ Russian Travel:
1-404-827-0099

CHAPTER 4

Health Matters: Clinics and Physicians Offering Services in English

Don't underestimate travel insurance. One of the best available resources offering a comparison of existing policies can be found at **www.insuremytrip.com.** There are quotes for every budget and almost all the options include medical coverage.

A few friends of ours had to seek medical advice while traveling in Russia. Others had to explore Russian pharmacies looking for certain products and it was not easy. We did some research in this area and put together a few helpful hints, as well as some useful websites to consult.

The medical situation in Russia has greatly improved over the past years. You can now buy western quality pharmaceuticals in a drugstore ("Apteka" in Russian). Basic medical services are free in Russia but several private outpatient clinics and hospitals opened after perestroika. The medical and diagnostic equipment in these clinics is similar to that of American facilities. Several clinics in Moscow and St Petersburg are staffed with European- and American-trained physicians. The American Medical

Center (AMC) is one of such ventures. Some clinics accept American insurance.

In some situations a patient might require medical evacuation. With that in mind it would be a good idea to choose an insurance policy with that option. You could also choose to buy a membership with the American Medical Center for the duration of your trip. Although not required for traveling to Russia, it is always a good idea to be up to date with vaccinations. The Tick-Born Encephalitis vaccination is recommended when traveling to the forest areas, since Russia has a high rate of Lyme disease.

The website **www.Russianadoption.org** (Click on "*Vaccination for Travelers to Russia*") offers an overview of health concerns in Russia and many links to other resources for health and travel provided by Russian, American and Canadian physicians who have been working in Moscow for several years.

www.gateway2russia.com has the most up-to-date information on Russian society and its economy, and is an important resource for information on the country's markets, corporations and regions. In the section, "*Your visit to Russia*", information on American and European medical clinics in Moscow and St. Petersburg, as well as their emergency numbers, can be found.

Another interesting website is **http://stpetersburg.usconsulate.gov.** Click on "*American Citizens Services*", then on the section "*Useful Information*", and scroll down to "*Medical List*". It gives a comprehensive summary of St. Petersburg's western medical clinics with details on the physicians' credentials, house calls, 24-hour availability and emergency care.

NATIONAL EMERGENCY PHONE NUMBERS IN RUSSIA:

Emergency	01
Police	02
Ambulance	03

MOSCOW EMERGENCY NUMBERS

Emergency Public Safety Center in Moscow (495)-937-9911
English Language Emergency Service (495)-257-4503 or 257-4509
Psychiatric ambulance in Moscow (495) 625-3101

Contagious Disease Ambulance (495) 208-9425

ST. PETERSBURG EMERGENCY NUMBER FOR ENGLISH SPEAKING VISITORS -

(812) 164-9787

MEDICAL SERVICES FOR INTERNATIONAL VISITORS IN MOSCOW (ENGLISH SPEAKING PERSONNEL)

Emergency services/ambulances:

American Medical Center	(495) 933-7700
American Hospital in Moscow	(495) 933-7700
European Medical center	(495) 933-6655
Medexpress	(495) 401-0382

HOSPITALS AND MEDICAL CENTERS WITH WESTERN-TRAINED PHYSICIANS AND EQUIPMENT

(See complete list in Supplement 2)

- **American Medical Center Moscow**: Open 24/7. Website **www.amcenter.ru** Click on the American flag in the right corner for the English version. E-mail: **info@amcenter.ru** Tel. (495) 933-7700
- **European Medical Center/European Surgical Center**: 24/7. Tel.: (495) 933-6655. Website: **www.emcmos.ru**
- **European Dental Center**: Tel. (495) 933-0002 Tel. (495) 933-6655
- **International SOS** 24-hour Alarm Center: Open 24/7 Tel. (495) 937-6477
- **International SOS** Clinic: Tel. (495) 937-5760 Emergency Tel. (495) 937-6477
- **Russian-American Family Medicine Center**: Tel. (495) 250-0646
- **European Medical Center**: Tel. (495) 797-5959
- **Canadian Family Clinic Mediclub**: Tel. (495) 931-5018

In the event of an emergency, the U.S. Embassy will try to assist in arranging medical care for U.S. citizens. For assistance during working hours, you can call (495)-728-5577. After 6.00 p.m., call the Embassy duty officer at (495)-728-5000.

Medical Services for International Visitors in St. Petersburg (English speaking personnel; for complete list see Supplement 2)

- **American Medical Clinic:** (AMC): 24/7. Tel. (812) 740-2090
  Website: **www. amclinic.ru**
- **EuroMed Clinic:** 24/7. Tel. (812) 327-0301
  Website: **www.euromed.ru**
- **The International Clinic MEDEM:** 24/7. Tel. (812) 336-3333
  Website: **www.medem.ru**

All of the above clinics have ambulance vehicles better equipped and staffed than the municipal ambulances. The direct line for AMC's ambulance service in St Petersburg is: (812) 164-9787. The medical staff speaks English.

PHARMACIES (APTEKA)

IN MOSCOW

One of the most popular health and beauty retailers is the Russian Pharmacy Chain called **36.6**. As you may know, **36.6** is the ideal body temperature in Centigrade (Celsius) for healthy adults and children. The company pioneered doctors' offices (GP's) in all their pharmacies. They went public with the first retail IPO in Russian history. Their Blue Logo can be seen all over Moscow and their numbers are growing fast. Apteka **36.6** provides excellent customer service and offers many American and European pharmaceuticals and over-the-counter medications, cosmetics, facial care products, etc.

Another popular pharmacy chain is called **Rigla**. A lot of their stores are offering 24-hour services.

Drug Store House: 4 Dobrininsky pereulok. Tel. (495) 237-4034

Pharmakon Drug Store: 4 Tverskaya Street. Tel. (495) 292-0843

IN ST PETERSBURG

American Medical Center Pharmacy:10 Serpukhovskaya Street.
Tel. (812) 326-1730

Petropharm pharmacy: 22 Nevsky prospect, open 24 hours.
Telephone (812)-314-5401 or nightline at (812) 311-2077

International pharmacy Damian: 22 Moskovskiy Prospect.
Tel. (812) 110-1744

HOW TO FIND OVER-THE-COUNTER AND FIRST-AID MEDICATION

Although medications available throughout the world are sometimes made of the same ingredients and have different brand names, their generic names remain the same. It is always recommended to travel with your own medication. In an emergency situation, you will find your medicine in any country of the world under its generic name. If you need a prescription contact one of the clinics listed above.

Here are some over-the-counter medications and their international equivalents:

Tylenol (*acetaminophen*) = **Paracetamol** (*acetaminophen*)
Motrin (*ibuprofen*) = **Nurofen forte** (*ibuprofen*)
Maalox antacid = **Maalox** (*aluminum and magnesium hydroxide*)
Robitussin and **Robitussin Plus** = **Tussin** and **Tussin Plus** syrup (*dextromethorphan and Guaiphenesin* common contents)
Claritin (*loratadine*) = **Klaritin** (*loratadine*)
Aspirin (*acetylsalicylic acid*) = **Aspirin** (*acetylsalicylic acid)*

TRAVELER'S DIARRHEA

People often want to know how to prevent or treat Traveler's diarrhea.

We consulted the best sources, i.e. pharmacists and doctors, and found that there are a few golden rules to abide by:

1. Do not drink tap water. Buy bottled water instead.
2. Wash your hands, peel fruit, and eat thoroughly cooked food.

However if you experience diarrhea, here are some over the counter products:

Pepto-Bismol, Kaopectate, Loperamide (Imodium), **Probiotics** such as, **Culturelle** and **Florastor**. Consult your physician prior to departure which medications to take with you.

We sincerely hope that you will not have to use the information in this chapter during your travels, however we feel it is essential to be prepared.

CHAPTER 5

Home Away from Home: Finding the Right Accommodation

WELL-HIDDEN LOCAL SECRETS

Millions of travelers would like to experience a new country by getting a taste of its authentic local life. It is not a new trend in the travelers' world and you have to admit it is an exciting choice. Why book a hotel when you can find an apartment for the same price and sometimes less. More space and a fully equipped kitchen would be a nice bonus. Apartment living offers the luxury of home comfort in a foreign country. With an opportunity to dive head first into the local culture, why spoil it by staying in a boring hotel room. Besides, Moscow's room prices, especially in centrally located hotels, range from $300.00 a night at the Marriott to $900.00 dollars a night at the Ritz Carlton. Rather than spending money in restaurants, you could be cooking in your own apartment kitchen. Fresh produce and mouth watering authentic Russian food can be found in any neighborhood. With the money you'll save you can splurge on sightseeing and gifts. If you enjoy the experience of apartment living, you might never go back to staying in hotels.

TIPS ON PUBLIC TRANSIT

When looking for an apartment, make sure the area you choose is safe, secure, and central. Moscow and St Petersburg are big cities and the best way to get around is by subway, or *Metro*, as Russians call their underground transportation system. When choosing your location ask how long it takes to get to the city center by Metro. It should not be longer than a twenty-minute ride and your apartment should be an easy five-minute walk to the Metro station. Other available means of transportation are trams, electric streetcars, buses and shuttles or 15-passenger mini vans.

The Moscow Metro is the best in the world; yet, it is a good idea to take a look at the metro map before you jump in. The lines are color-coded. Most major stations are hubs for easy transfers. They are spacious, and lavishly decorated.

Renting a car might not be the smartest idea since Moscow traffic jams have long put Los Angeles, New York and Miami to shame. However, if you enjoy driving in Paris, Rome and Athens, you probably won't be intimidated by the aggressive, obnoxious, and at times, suicidal style of Moscow drivers.

TAXIS IN ST. PETERSBURG AND MOSCOW

Multilingual operators are available at **www.taxi-service.spb.ru.** You can also call St. Petersburg Taxi at 7-921-374-9444. You should avoid unlicensed taxi drivers who solicit at the gate. They are on the lookout for unsuspecting tourists and your taxi ride may become overly expensive. One of the widely used websites that gets great reviews can be found at **www.gotoru.com.** You can actually reserve a taxi before you even leave the United States. The Moscow office can be reached at 7-495-730-5477 and the St. Petersburg office phone number is 7-812-324-4190. A licensed taxi service in Sheremetievo Airport (SVO) is located at the arrival level. Before paying for the taxi, refer to the city map to determine the distance and the price. Rates may vary from $50.00 to $70.00 (1300 - 1700 rubles) per ride depending on the city zone. All taxi rides are prepaid. **Waytorussia.net** also provides car service. You can read reviews of their services on their website if you click on the link *Transport/Taxi Page.*

TRANSPORTATION TIPS: FIND WHAT YOU NEED

1. What size car can I book for the number of people traveling with me, and all the luggage we have?

Helpful hint: Ask for a van if you have a lot of luggage. Many Russian and European cars are less spacious than American cars.

2. What is the phone number for an English-speaking taxi service in case the reserved car does not show up?

Helpful hint: Be sure to obtain all the necessary details, i.e. location and time to meet with the rental agent. This information is vital if the reserved car does not show up.

HOW TO CHOOSE THE RIGHT APARTMENT

Finding the right apartment might be a challenge for virgin travelers especially if they do not speak the language or understand the culture of the place. Here we will provide you with a few tips on how to find an apartment, what to look for and what questions to ask when communicating with rental agencies. Go on-line, check the websites, read comments and complaints about the service, then send an email or call them directly. Check if the agency has an office in the U.S. Have they worked with American tourists before and do they have any idea of what American travelers expect? Even if you are a savvy traveler ready to face any challenge, be prepared for surprises, big or small.

Read the apartment's description, and make sure you really understand how many bedrooms it has. Americans usually describe their dwellings as one-, two- and three-bedroom apartments. Russians always refer to one-, two- or three-room apartments. A Russian three-room apartment usually has two bedrooms, a living room and a kitchen, which also serves as a dining room. The living room is often furnished with a hide-away sofa bed, and if you get the chance, check to see if it is comfortable enough to sleep on. Ask about the bed sizes, and if you are taller than 6'2" expect your bed to be a little short. If you happen to get a luxurious mattress, consider yourself lucky. Some agencies renovate potential rental units to turn them into standard American-like apartments. If you are not sure about the description on the Internet, ask the agency to describe the sleeping arrangements in detail. Once we had ended up in an apartment in Moscow where the second bedroom was a den. It had a twin size bed with a very poor mattress and a baby crib next to it. In reality, there was only one bedroom with a queen size bed. King size beds are still a rarity not only in Russia but also in Europe in general. Europeans do not believe in super size yet. To sum it up, when renting an apartment, carefully check out the sleeping arrangements.

AIR-CONDITIONING

Americans believe that Russia is a cold and snowy place. Very few realize that the country embraces 11 time zones with diverse climates. It is true that winters in Moscow and St Petersburg can be quite cold, and summers are hot and short. Always check the average temperatures in the area you plan to travel to. If you are traveling in the summer, ask your agency if the rental unit has an air-conditioner. For example, in June the temperature can climb to between 30-32C (86-89F) in St. Petersburg, 35C (95F) in Moscow, and 36-37C (96.8- 98.6F) in Tomsk, Central Siberia. Wall-mounted air conditioners with a remote control are quite common in Russia.

WHAT YOU NEED TO KNOW ABOUT APARTMENT BATHROOMS AND OTHER FACILITIES

Many apartments in Russia have a separate small bathroom with a tub or a shower and an even smaller toilet. Travelers usually find this arrangement quite convenient when several people share the same apartment. Modern apartment buildings are equipped with western style bathrooms with a tub/shower and a toilet in one room. Ask if your bathroom has centralized water heating or an independently controlled boiler. It is very common in Russia and some other European countries to shut off the central heating system for a couple of weeks during the summer for maintenance. Most of the renovated rental apartments will have a separate water heater for your shower. Always ask your host to provide detailed instructions on how to use it. If the bathroom is part of the central water heating system, check when the hot water is to be cut off. A rental company can find the maintenance schedule. There's usually a front-loading washing machine in the bathroom or kitchen. It spins clothes to the state of "almost dry" which is the main reason why the dryers are seldom used. Check if the apartment has either a clothesline or a rack. Russian bathrooms have towel warmers where you can hang your clothes to dry. If you can't live without a coffee maker, you will be disappointed. Do not expect to see a regular coffee maker in a Russian kitchen. They are not popular in Europe. Russians, like many Europeans, prefer to drink instant coffee or tea in the morning and then go out to a coffee shop to have a good cup of coffee and meet friends. You will most probably find an electric kettle. If you decide you still want to make a fresh cup of coffee, we recommend that you take a look at a French press or an espresso maker at **www.espressozone.com** or **www.liquidplanet.com.** You can also ask the rental agency to buy one for the apartment and coffee is always available in local grocery stores. You can also find different brands of loose tea or tea bags in the stores. Ask the rental agency for a complete list of kitchen appliances and accessories.

SECURITY SYSTEM IN YOUR APARTMENT

Rental apartments in Russia may have double doors and multiple locks. The apartment building usually has a central code for the front door, which prevents unauthorized entry. This code will be provided to you by the agency. It's in the rental agency's best interest to keep you safe by choosing a secure apartment in a safe part of the city. You can ask for an apartment on a higher floor if it will make you feel safer, but don't forget to ask if the building has a functioning elevator.

INTERNET, PHONE AND OTHER MEANS OF COMMUNICATION

A free Internet WiFi service is offered by most rental agencies. When checking in, ask your host if the Internet connection works. It is important to get as much information as possible from the agency's representative while he is still in the apartment with you. Also make sure that the phone in the apartment is in service and what the call restrictions are. Be sure to secure several emergency phone numbers to reach the agents and verify that they will be able to communicate with you in English.

A GSM phone might be something to consider (see chapter on cell phones).

QUESTIONS WORTH ASKING

1. Where is

- the closest grocery store, a pharmacy or a drug store (Apteka in Russian)?
- a cell phone store to purchase SIM cards or calling cards?
- an Internet café and a WiFi location?
- a restaurant?
- a taxi service with English speaking personnel?

2. Where can I get a city map?
3. How and where can I buy tickets for local transportation?
4. Is the apartment equipped with English cable TV?
5. Make your own list of questions.

APARTMENT HUNTING IN MOSCOW, ST. PETERSBURG, AND OTHER RUSSIAN AND UKRAINIAN CITIES. USEFUL WEBSITES

One of the best information resources about traveling to Russia can be found at **www.waytorussia.net.** This is a resource website founded and run by two young Russian entrepreneurs. They do not provide services but have contracts with travel companies and rental agencies in Moscow, St. Petersburg, Novosibirsk, Ekaterinburg, and Riga, Latvia. The Waytorussia team provides an objective and detailed analysis of apartments with all their pros and cons. They understand the needs of American and European tourists and they send their representatives to inspect each rental unit. On this website you will also find practical tips on what each area has to offer.

Another useful site is **www.gotorussia.com** or their affiliated company at **www.apartmentres.com.** You can take a virtual tour of an apartment and read its description. The company offers transportation from the airport to the apartment for an extra fee and gives you a discount if you rent online. The company has offices in Atlanta, San Francisco, and Moscow.

Another website worth looking at is **www.enjoymoscow.com,** hosted by Rick Moncher, an American living in Moscow. Rick is married to a Russian woman who speaks fluent English and helps him run the business. The website provides virtual tours of the units and good pictures of the apartments owned by the company. The description is detailed and clear. Rick will also rent you a cell phone for the duration of your stay. Their service is 24/7 in English and Russian and they can also help you register your visa for a $50.00 fee. For St. Petersburg's rentals see their website at **www.nevsky88.com**. Most apartments are studios and one-bedroom flats. Read the reviews for more details.

Here are some more websites to explore while looking for apartments:

- **www.aventec.ru**
- **www.flatlink.ru**
- **www.kalitagrad.ru**
- **www.likehome.ru**
- **www.moscowapartments4u.com**
- **www.enjoymoscow.com**

If you prefer to live in apartments while traveling in Europe, whether it's in Italy or the Czech Republic, France or Russia, be prepared for the unexpected such as: your airport pick-up not showing up; your agent who has the house key not being on time; no hot water; or a warm refrigerator. Have your cell phone programmed with emergency numbers, find out how to wave down a cab (Russian style), and find out where the nearest Laundromat is and the services it provides. Remember to laugh at life's little quirks; that's what the Russians do.

CHAPTER 6

How to Stay Connected: Cell Phones, Calling Cards and Internet

If you plan to travel in Europe, you may consider using a GSM phone. GSM stands for Global System of Mobile Communications. They are commonly known as *world phones* and have become the most popular standard phones in Europe and in many countries around the world. T-mobile, AT&T (Cingular) and Verizon sell GSM phones that can function inside and outside of the USA.

WHY DO YOU NEED A CELL PHONE ABROAD?

You already know the answer. That's right, it makes your trip so much easier. From the airport, you can get in touch with the apartment rental company; while on the train between two cities, you can book tickets to the show you have just read about; you can make an emergency phone call; and your friends and family can always reach you.

GSM phones and networks do not operate on the same frequency bands in the USA and abroad. While North American phones use 850MHz and 1900MHz, the European ones use 900MHz and 1800 MHz. The 850Mhz band is also used in Australia, Canada, and many South American countries. In order for your phone to operate properly, it has to be compatible with the network provider.

Dual Band, TriBand and Quad Band phones, presently available on the market, operate on two, three, or all four frequency ranges. When buying a Dual or a TriBand phone, make sure you find out what frequency ranges it is compatible with. Then go to **www.gsmworld.com** to find the country of your destination in the GSM roaming section. Check the frequency range for the GSM phone systems, and then get the phone that suits your travel needs. Most of the countries outside of the USA use a 900/1800 MHz or a 2100 3G fast connection system. Be aware that 900 MHz is more popular than 1800 MHz, but if all this sounds too complicated, just go ahead and buy a quad phone.

The GSM World company website **www.gsmworld.com** is a great source of information on GSM Operators, Coverage Maps and Roaming Information.

LOCKED/UNLOCKED PHONES

When you buy a GSM phone, make sure you get an unlocked one, which allows you to use any provider's SIM card. Most wireless companies "lock" their phones, i.e. program them in such a way that the phones can only operate with their SIM cards. However, if you have a locked GSM phone, there is a way to have it unlocked. Having a phone unlocked has become easier since the U.S. Copyright Office declared in November 2006 that consumers could not be prosecuted for unlocking a phone that they own and signing up with another carrier. You can ask your provider to unlock your GSM phone. T-Mobile has the friendliest unlocking policy and AT&T Wireless will unlock customers' phones only after the contract is over (1- 2 years). David M. Rowell, a commentator on **www.thetravelinsider.com**, provides tips on unlocking GSM phones and offers a great overview on World Phones, as well as any other technology available today for travelers. David was quoted in *USA Today* on the subject on World phones.

A heated discussion came up about unlocking phones after instructions on how to unlock the iPhone were published on the Internet. It will be interesting to see what happens next. We can only hope that it will become common practice for wireless service providers in the USA to sell unlocked phones, just like it is in other countries around the globe.

WHERE TO BUY A GSM PHONE

GSM phone prices can vary between $90 and $500.

T-Mobile, Cingular (AT&T), and Verizon offer their own (locked) GSM phones.

Different models of unlocked GSM phones may be purchased on E-bay and Amazon. Make sure the phone charger works with both 110 and 240 volts.

Telestial.com and **Cellularabroad.com** also sell unlocked GSM phones, SIM cards, and international calling cards. They offer special package deals (phone and SIM).

Check out **www.mobal.com** because on this website you can buy inexpensive cell phones and services, your assigned phone number never expires, and you are charged on a per call basis. However, their rates are much higher compared to other SIM card sellers.

SIM CARDS

If you purchase a GSM phone, you will need a SIM card; which is a small chip to insert into your phone. Without a SIM card, a GSM phone is an empty shell. This removable chip contains your phone number, subscription details, and identifies the network. The same SIM card can be used with any unlocked GSM phone, and some SIM cards function in more than one country.

You can use the SIM card from your current service provider: T-Mobile, AT&T, or Verizon. These companies have international calling plans and charge $1.25- $5.00 /min. You will be charged for all incoming phone calls as well.

We believe that the best solution is to buy a local SIM card with a local phone number. In Russia we recommend either Megafone, Beeline, or MTS. Your local calls will be quite affordable and incoming calls are free, but check the rates for international calls, since prices may vary.

Having a local phone number would not only be economical for you but for your old and new Russian friends as well; since they would not be calling long distance to speak to you. It is a nice gesture.

A Megaphone SIM card can be purchased online through Telestial, Cellularabroad as well as a number of other companies on the Internet. If you arrive without a SIM card, you can buy one in a local Megafone, Beeline or MTS store. Visit "*TalkLounge*" at **www.waytorussia.net** to read more on "Where to buy SIM cards for Russia".

You can also save money on international phone calls from your cell/home/office phone, by using a prepaid calling card. The cost of phone calls using pre-paid cards are amazingly cheap: $0.03 - $0.05 per minute. This can be a great alternative, but it may also prove to be a little inconvenient to dial multiple numbers when you're in a hurry.

A SIM card is usually deactivated some time after 6 months and you may lose the unused minutes. To keep the SIM card "alive" you must keep using it. For more details, check the company requirements. Lending your card to a friend going on a trip during these months is a good way to keep your SIM card active.

REFILLING YOUR SIM CARD

If you run out of prepaid time on your SIM card, you can buy a refill in a local cell phone store where you can speak to a specialist. When you purchase a multi-country SIM card, consult their website to find out if the card can be refilled, and if you can pay with your credit card.

RENTING A GSM PHONE

Check the fees, and weigh the pros and cons before renting a phone. It might be less expensive to buy a phone and a SIM card.

However, if you decide to rent a GSM phone, consult the following websites:

- **www.telestial.com**
- **www.cellularabroad.com**
- **www.smartcoms.com**
- **www.worldroam.com**

If you are dealing with a management company for your lodging accommodations it might be possible to rent a GSM phone from them. You should check that out.

The following websites offer valuable information:

- **www.thetravelinsider.com** - Unlocking GSM phones, updates on technology, and general information for travelers.
- **www.waytorussia.net** - Visit their discussion board "*Talk Lounge*".
- **www.slowtrav.com** - Click on "*Forums*" and find "*Technology at Home and On the Go*", where travelers share their stories about cell phones, computers, laptops, GSM, photo cameras, video cameras and much more. With a SlowTrav membership, you can get discounts on cell phones from Telestial and Cellularabroad.
- **www.telestial.com** - Offers cell phones and SIM cards, calling cards, and electric adapters for travel outside of the U.S. It offers attractive promotions.
- **www.cellularabroad.com** - Provides services similar to Telestial.
- **www.wtng.info** (recommended by Slowtrav.com) This is a world telephone number guide on how to dial different countries.
- **www.timeanddate.com/worldclock** - Provides world clock and time zones. It calculates the time difference with other corners of the world by comparing it to your computer clock.
- **www.intellicast.com** - Weather for active travelers.
- **www.voltagevalet.com** - Travelers' choice for dual voltage travel appliances, converters, adaptors and much more.
- **www.gsmworld.com** - All about GSM bands.

NEW SOLUTIONS TO STAYING IN TOUCH

More recently people have been contracting the services of companies that use Voice over Internet Protocol (VoIP) software to route international calls through home computers. These companies are Vonage (**www.vonage.com**) and Skype (**www.skype.com**). Most of the VoIP providers have low per-minute charges for international calls. Our favorite is Skype, which offers free communication between Skype users. If you travel with your laptop, the only thing you need is a high-speed Internet connection and a microphone. Download the Skype software from their website before the trip. It is free of charge and user friendly.

The SkypeOut service allows you to call a landline or a mobile phone from your computer. Deposit money in your Skype account and you can make phone calls around the world. SkypeOut offers the following rates for Russia:

- To Moscow $0.021/min
- To St Pete $0.021/min
- To Russia (outside of above cities) $0.048/min
- To Cell phones $0.071/min

(Note: Rates are subject to change)

Skype's popularity has skyrocketed over the last few years. Skype is a very dynamic company that improves and updates its services on a regular basis.

However, we still encourage our readers to do their own research to find the right VoIP service based on their specific needs.

The following companies are not VOIP:

WDT (World Discount Telecommunications) offers a **Dial Around Service,** also called a Toll Free Access Number Service. Upon signing up, you will receive an access number. You will be billed only when you make a call. The company offers great international rates. Calls to Russia cost:

- Moscow $0.025/min
- St Pete $0.025/min
- Russia $0.059/min
- Mobile $0.119/min

(Note: Rates are subject to change)

The WDT Website - **www.mywdt.com.**

Check **www.startec.com** for similar services and competitive rates for calls to Moscow, St Petersburg and other Russian cities.

While we have attempted to provide the most up-to-date information, the world of technology changes rapidly. The purpose of this book is to refer you to the best web sources for information on how to plan your trip.

CHAPTER 7

Nurture Your Curiosity: Moscow, St. Petersburg and Beyond

This chapter consists of three parts. In the first, we focused on some of our favorite places in Moscow, where we love to take our American friends. The second part has some suggestions on how to plan a trip to St. Petersburg. In the third part we talk about other places that are worth visiting in Russia.

NOT-TO-MISS PLACES AND EVENTS IN MOSCOW

Besides the usual places of interest that most tourists visit in Moscow, such as the Kremlin, the Red Square, the Tretyakov Galery, the Pushkin Museum, St Basil's Cathedral and GUM (The Central Department Store in Red Square), and the Novodevichy Convent and Cemetery, the city offers a variety of other attractions that are not on the first tier list. In a city of rich culture and tradition, there are numerous hidden treasures and special seasonal events. During some free time on a lazy afternoon, wouldn't you like to get a taste of Russian tradition? Here are some suggestions:

The New Building of the Tretyakov Gallery (also known as the House of Artists). The main exhibition is of 1900 contemporary art, including such internationally known artists as Shagall, Kandinsky, Malevich, etc. There are also many concessions selling arts and crafts, jewelry, paintings and prints. This is a great place to buy souvenirs as well as art. To plan your visit, consult **www.tretyakovgallery.ru** (English version).

Open: 10.00 a.m. - 7.30 p.m. Closed on Mondays. Metro Park Kulturi, Red line and Oktiabrskaya, Circular Brown line.

Kolomenskoye is an imperial estate near Moscow where in 1532 the Church of the Ascension was built to celebrate the birth of the prince who was later to become known as Tsar Ivan IV (the Terrible). It is located on a steep bank of the Moscow River surrounded by 390 hectares of old forest and is now one of the UNESCO's World Heritage Sites. Kolomenskoe Park is a favorite among Moscovites for sun bathing and horseback riding in the summer, as well as snowy walks and sleigh rides in the winter.

Rides along the Moscow River in a stylized wooden boat accompanied by live folk music are available. Museum cafeterias serve traditional Russian hot tea, blintzes and pancakes.

Open: 11.00 a.m. - 5.00 p.m. Closed on Mondays. Metro Kolomenskaya, Green line.

All-Russian Exhibition Center (Vserosiyskiy Vistavochniy Centre – VVC), formerly known as VDNKh, is a permanent trade show. The 586.6 square acre property is used as a recreational park, and besides the trade center, the park has numerous exhibition halls. Some pavilions house Russian and international exhibits but in most pavilions you will find vendors selling everything imaginable, from hi-tech gadgets to inexpensive household items made in China. In the summer, the park is transformed into a huge gorgeous garden with various attractions, park rides and breathtaking fountains. In the winter, there are sleigh rides and a magnificent ice sculpture exhibit. There is no entrance fee and the Center is open daily. The website address is **www.vvcentre.ru** (click on English version at the top).

The grounds are open: 9.00 a.m. - 6.00 p. m. on weekdays and 9.00 a.m. -7.00 p.m. on weekends. The exhibition halls are open: 10.00 a.m. – 5.00 p.m. Metro VDNKh, Orange line.

Moscow Botanical Garden borders on the All-Russian Exhibition Center. The Garden hosts over 16 thousand species of plants from all over the world, a Japanese garden, and a rose garden with 20 thousand rose bushes. The garden is worth visiting during spring and summer when the weather is good.

Open: 10.00 a.m. – 6.00 p.m. (winter), 10.00 a.m. – 8.00 p.m. (summer). Closed on Mondays. Entrance is free. Metro Vladikino, Grey line.

The Museum of Private Collections opened in 1985. It houses 12 private collections of 16th-20th century Russian art, as well as some pieces of Western fine art. The permanent exhibition on the ground floor boasts of several personal effects and various drawings belonging to Salvador Dali and Henri Matisse. The 3rd floor hosts a Russian collection by the famous 19th century artists Borovikovskii, Repin, Serov, Benua, and Vrubel, as well as many Russian icons from the 16th - 17th centuries. The 4th floor features an impressive display of 20th century Russian art.

Open: Noon - 7.00 p.m. from Wednesday to Sunday. The museum is closed on the last Friday of every month. Entrance fee: 50 rubles. Metro: Kropotkinskaya, Red line, 14, Volkhonka Street.

Sanduny Bath House: The Russian Banya is an old Russian tradition. It is somewhat similar to a Finish Sauna but with a lot of hot steam. Sanduny is one of the oldest and most beautiful bathhouses in Russia. Built like a palace, the building dates back to 1896. The marble staircase alone is worth a visit. In 2004 both the Banya and its restaurant were renovated in accordance with the original 19th century plans. You can book an individual excursion of the Banya and enjoy a 2-hr session in the baths followed by a delicious Russian dinner at the restaurant. Read more about Sanduny at **www.sanduny.ru/en.**

We have talked about only a fraction of what can be found on the Moscow side venues. These are places where we took our American friends and they absolutely loved the experience. We are happy to share them with you.

If you would like more information on the above-mentioned places, consult **www.waytorussia.net** or their team via email or blogs. They offer a tour guide and transportation. We have mentioned this website several times because the team is made up of dedicated promoters of travel to Russia and their company employs dynamic young people who love their country.

ST. PETERSBURG HINTS

St. Petersburg is the former Imperial capital of Russia, built by Peter the Great, and one of the major tourist destinations in the Russian Federation. Abundant information on its history, sights, and places to stay is available in most bookstores and on the Internet, however, to narrow down your search, we recommend focusing on a few websites created by several Russian companies in St. Petersburg. Local sources of information are usually more authentic and detailed.

www.Petersburgcity.com offers extensive information about the history and culture of the city, its surroundings, accommodations, dining, and sightseeing tours. It also offers playbill information, shopping, museums, events, and other useful tips.

Take a look at the Tourism section to learn about the suburbs (or *environs,* as they call them) like Valaam, Krondshtadt, Vyborg, Oranienbaum, Gatchina, and Pavlovsk. You might decide to visit the towns of Pushkin and Peterhoff, where the old Royal summer residences are situated, or better yet, go to Strelna to see the Konstantinovsky Palace, which President Putin has transformed into Palace of Congresses.

Interested in visiting museums? The Culture section gives you names and descriptions of every museum in town, including the Fedor Dostoevsky Literary and Memorial Museum, the Alexander Pushkin Apartment Museum, and the Cabin of Peter the Great.

Want to enjoy Russian Ballet or the Philharmonic? The Theater section will have an event for you. Before visiting the Hermitage Fine Arts Museum, explore their website **www.hermitagemuseum.org.**

www.rus-ballet.com is owned by and dedicated to two ballet companies: the Imperial Hermitage Theater and the Palace Theater.

www.visitrussia.com or **www.balletandopera.com** offer on-line ticket reservations to the theaters of Moscow and St. Petersburg. Both companies have box offices in Russia, or the US, or the UK.

www.rus-tours.com is owned by Eridan, a Russian company based in St. Petersburg. It offers excursions in and out of the city in a car of your choice, as well as river cruises or boat excursions along the city's numerous canals. Newly opened to tourists are the Konstantinovsky Palace, mentioned above, Shuvalovka, and Gatchina.

Want to visit the graves of some famous people like Dostoevsky, Tchaikovsky, Glinka, and Rimsky-Korsakov, or the first Mayor of Saint Petersburg Anatoly Sobchak? They can be found at the Tikhvin Cemetery, located in the Alexander Nevsky Monastery.

The Piskaryosvskoye Memorial Cemetery, located on Unvanquished Avenue, is dedicated to the victims of the Leningrad Siege. Read more on **www.wikipedia.org.**

All of the above listed resources will help you plan an exciting and agreeable trip to Russia's Crown Jewel City.

SPECIAL EVENTS

New Year's and Christmas all over Russia is a time for the Russian Winter Festival. In Moscow and St. Petersburg the festival starts on New Year's Eve and lasts up to 10 days. The celebration continues well into Old Style Christmas festivities, which are held on January 7, according to the Russian Orthodox tradition. There are many parties, folk and classical music shows, troika (three-horse) sleigh rides, masquerades, dances, balls, food markets, and singing. Major city squares host special festive events. During the week of celebrations there are numerous skiing and skating contests, sports events and Christmas shows. For several years Russians have been enjoying a long public holiday at this time of the year.

Maslennitsa is a one-week traditional Russian folk festival, celebrating the end of winter and the beginning of Lent, much like Mardi Gras in other parts of the world. Since perestroika, this festival has been celebrated on a grand scale all over the country. The highlight of the week is a carnival parade in downtown Moscow and St. Petersburg. There are countless traditional foods and drinks, art and craft fairs, singing, dancing, fun games, contests, raffles, etc. If you are in Russia at this time of year, it is not an event to miss.

White Nights Festival is a special time to visit St. Petersburg. The phenomenon of white nights lasts from mid-May to July in this northern Russian city, and during this time the sun never sets. Since 1993, St Petersburg's famous Mariinsky Opera and Ballet Theatre has hosted an annual festival: **The Stars of the White Nights**. The festival's program includes concerts at Mariinsky Theatre, as well as outdoor events in the parks, small theatres, and public courtyards. The city comes alive with music and its bars and restaurants never close for the night during the festival. It is a great time to visit the city and to experience its culture. Read more about the festival at **www.en.wikipedia.org.**

PLACES TO VISIT IN OTHER PARTS OF RUSSIA

Besides Moscow and St Petersburg, there are several popular travel destinations worth considering. The Golden Ring, River Cruises, and the Trans-Siberian Express are some of them. Here is a brief description of these destinations and some websites to consult.

The Golden Ring is a group of towns; they are Vladimir, Suzdal, Kostroma, Yaroslavl, Rostov, Pereslavl-Zalesskiy, and Sergeiev Posad. There are many restored churches, monasteries, fortresses, museums, and wooden villages to visit. The WaytoRussia Agency believes that it is possible to visit all seven cities in 8 days. The website has information on these destinations, maps, distances between the cities, and what there is to see. The website also allows you to calculate travel costs and provides answers to many questions; the rest is up to you. Historical details about the Golden Ring can be found in such travel books as Lonely Planet and Rough Guide to Russia

River Cruising is an excellent way to observe Russia's treasure, its magnificent display of nature. The cruise ship will dock in old cities like Uglitch, Yaroslavl, Goritsky, and Kiji Island, all in the vicinities of St. Petersburg. The duration of the cruise depends on its destination. Most of them last from 3 to 12 days. Cruises are offered from the end of May till the end of September and ships sail between Moscow and St. Petersburg. Refer to the following websites for further information: **www.visitrussia.com** and **www.wayto-russia.net. Visitrussia** has an office in New York City.

The Trans-Siberian Express: Jump on the Trans-Siberian Express to see Siberia and the Russian Far East in one trip. It is every foreigner's dream. The Trans-Siberian Railroad is the longest railroad on Earth. Lake Baikal, Ulan Ude in Buryatia, and Vladivostok are located along the way and the train crosses nine time zones. Siberia is a beautiful land of cold winters and short hot summers. Not many people realize how beautiful this land really is. A short Siberian summer is an explosion of taste and color. It is a land where Nature tries to catch up with the intensity of life after a long winter. The Trans-Siberian Rail Odysseys are offered by

- Mir Corporation at **www.mircorp.com**
- Express to Russia at **www.expresstorussia.com**
- The Great Canadian Travel Company at **www.greatcanadiantravel.com** (See the section on Russia and the Orient train at **www.travel333.com**

Sochi, 2014 Winter Olympic destination, known as the Russian Riviera, is situated on the Black Sea in the subtropical climate zone against the backdrop of the Caucasus Mountain Range. Many countries had fought over this location in the past until it became part of Russia in 1829. Its Mediterranean style architecture prevails and there are many mineral springs and natural spas. The Botanical Garden, known as the Dendrarium, is a maze of secret gardens and areas that resemble the public spaces in Paris. The Fine Arts Exhibition Hall offers a magnificent collection of Russian art from the beginning of the 20th century. You might run into the Russian movie elite who are in town for the annual summer film festival Kinotavr. If you are there in the fall you should visit the famous Velvet Season Fashion Show.

From June through October the sea is warm enough for swimming. Wintertime temperatures range from the 40s to lower 50s. It is often sunny and humid and the Caucasus Mountains boast enough snow for winter sports. Visit **www.sochi2014.com** to read more about the current preparations for the Olympics.

Another interesting source of information on Sochi and its vicinities is **www.btgroup.ru**. You will appreciate an extensive list of hotels and their descriptions. The section named 'How to Get There' seems to be the most comprehensive we have found so far. It lists plane and train schedules as well as the special services offered in the VIP lounge at Adler Airport. Tourists may gain access to the VIP lounge by paying an additional fee.

How to get there: Take a plane to Moscow or St Petersburg. A connecting domestic flight will then take you to Adler (Utair, or Siberian airlines). Domestic flights and rates can be found at **www.visitrussia.com** or **www.btgroup.ru.**

Most of the above-mentioned destinations have been popular with tourists from all over the world; the information on these destinations is easy to find. In the next chapter, we will focus on less known destinations like Kamchatka, Lake Baikal, Elbrus, and the Altay Mountains. These destinations are mostly popular with 'adrenaline junkies'. Kayaking and rafting in white waters, bear watching, Siberian river fishing or exploring mountain peaks are just a few activities to consider.

CHAPTER 8

Explore Your Wild Side: Adventure Travel

Adventure, wilderness, and nature travel have continued to grow in popularity over the past years, forming a new niche in the travel industry. The stress of the work place and every day concerns make people anxious to reconnect with nature and admire its beauty and simplicity.

Russia offers numerous opportunities for nature travel. Since the fall of the Iron Curtain in 1991, the country has become more open, and travelers now get a chance to see and explore previously closed areas. Here are some of the most popular wilderness destinations:

- The Russian Far East: Kamchatka
- Siberia: Lake Baikal
- The South Central Russia: the Altay mountains
- The Caucuses: Elbrus
- The Northwest of Russia: Karelia

Kamchatka, known for its incredible pristine environment, is one of the prime areas that drew daring travelers from all over the world to the Russian Far East. Janet Waltham, a travel editor, wrote a vivid description of Kamchatka: "a hotbed of volcanic activity... the local ecology is a delicate mix of spectacular volcanoes and hot springs, glaciers, and ice fields. It is a travel destination with a difference, and the brown bear and the erupting volcano are just for starters. Hot water emerged as continuous fountains from a succession of spouters, and a handful of geysers periodically threw jets of boiling water and steam 10 or 20 m into the air. The colors are breathtaking: mineral deposits create brilliant red, green, and blue pools. The terraces are painted with orange streaks, and dumps of sulphur crystals gleam bright yellow in the sun".

PBS aired a wonderful presentation on Kamchatka and you can find a wealth of information on their website. Go to their search box, type in Kamchatka and enjoy the read. Another great description of Kamchatka, complemented by amazing photos is offered by Andrew Logan, a Kamchatkan traveler and fisherman. He provides a detailed and enlightening account of the peninsula in his article "The Ring of Fire". The article dwells on the geological history of the area and its volcanoes, a "never quiet" land, and describes animal life in a place where Earth is "still young".

Many companies offer trips to Kamchatka. One of them is *The Lost World*, founded in 1993 by Nikolay Kruglyakov, the head of Kamchatka's Alpine Rescue Service. The company offers a variety of trips for nature lovers and adventure travelers, such as wild salmon fishing, rafting with a possibility to observe brown bears, snowmobile tours to watch reindeer herds, skiing and dog sledding, mountaineering, boat rides, hot water spring viewings, and fall color viewing.

Wild Russia is another company offering Kamchatka tours since 1990. Their credits include consulting Outside Magazine on travel facilities and Condaneste Travel Magazine on journeys to Kamchatka. The company's noble cause is to promote socially and environmentally responsible travel, respect for local cultures, and giving back to the communities. "We recognize the human need for the quiet solitude and the beauty of the wilds. Wilderness is not a luxury, it's a necessity", says Yegor Churakov, the founder of the company.

Read more about Kamchatka at:

- **www.travelkamchatka.com** - The Lost World
- **www.pbs.org**
- **www.kamchatkapeninsula.com** - A. Logan article "The Ring of Fire"
- **www.wild-russia.org** - The Russian Nature Conservation Center

Here is a list of companies that offer trips to Kamchatka:

- **www.travelkamchatka.com** - Lost World
- **www.wildrussia.spb.ru** - Wild Russia
- **www.waytorussia.net** - Way to Russia
- **www.kamchatkatravel.net** - Beringia Company
- **www.kamchatkatracks.com** - Kamchatka Travel Group
- **www.kamchatbear.com** - Kamchatka Bear (click on the English version)

Lake Baikal is situated in Eastern Siberia. A true Russian jewel and one of the genuine seven natural wonders of the world, Lake Baikal is 395.1 miles long and 49.7 miles wide. Baikal's surface is the size of Maryland. It is one of the largest lakes in the world and is known to Russians as a Sacred Sea. The volume of water mass in this lake is greater than the water volume in all five Great Lakes in North America combined and it is the deepest lake on earth. The deepest spot ever found in the lake descends to 5370 feet. Baikal is the most ancient lake on our planet. It is nearly 25 million years old. To learn more about the Baikal geology and history go to **www.baikal.ru** and **www.wikipedia.com.**

There are several companies that offer a variety of tours around Lake Baikal. Tour options include rafting, kayaking, yacht sailing, cycling, horseback riding, and trekking. Winter tours include ice fishing, snowmobile rides, lake ice cycling, diving, skiing, and snowboarding. Tour durations may vary from 3 to 20 days. Taking into consideration the number of companies and their diverse interests, you will probably be able to find everything that the region has to offer. Here are some of the websites to explore:

- **www.waytorussia.net** - Type in *Irkutsk* and *Baikal* in a search window.
- **www.expresstorussia.com** - A Russian-American company with offices in Russia and the United States.
- **www.baikaltrekking.com** - A Russian company.
- **www.baikalcomplex.irk.ru** - A Russian company, Irkutsk.
- **www.mircorp.com** - Seattle, WA
- **www.cinderellatravel.com** - Rego Park, NY
- **www.baikalcomplex.com** - A Russian company, Irkutsk.
- **www.irkutsk-baikal.com** - A Russian company.
- **www.baikaler.com** and **www.baikalex.com** - Russian Baikal Tours.
- **www.mir-travel.com** - A Russian company, St. Petersburg.
- **www.geographicbureau.com** - A Russian company, St. Petersburg.
- **www.traveleastrussia.com** - Seattle, WA.

The Altay (Altai) is known as the Golden Mountains of Russia. The Altay mountain range is located within rich and diverse landscapes of steppe, taiga and semi-desert stretches from the Mongolia Gobi Desert to the West Siberian Plain. The range crosses Chinese, Mongolian, Russian and Kazakh lands. Altay is known for its mysterious rock drawings, mounds erected over tombs, and ancient archaeological treasures. Altay is hidden away from the industrial areas and is sparsely populated by native nomadic (Mongolian and Kazakh) inhabitants who have preserved a traditional way of life. Tourism and agriculture are the two main industries of the area.

Getting to the Altay mountains is not an easy task. Check **www.waytorussia.net** to learn more about this area and to find out how to get to this secluded area. Things to do in the Altay include climbing, mountaineering, trekking, hunting, rafting, paragliding, horseback riding, white water rafting, and cave exploring. The Altay region is internationally known for the Chuya Rafting Rally.

A California company called *Raft Siberia* is a great resource for information about Altay and rafting/kayaking expeditions. The company successfully operates rafting and kayaking expeditions along the rivers of the Altay Region and around Lake Baikal, building its reputation on its wealth of knowledge of the area. One of the founders, Valdimir Gavrilov, is a physicist and a whitewater expert. His book "Rivers of the Unknown Land" is a guide with detailed descriptions and river maps to whitewater regions in the former Soviet Union. You can buy the book on Amazon.com

A vast area of the Altay mountains including the Katun Natural Reserves, Lake Teletskoye, Mount Belukha, and the Ukok Plateau, is recognized by UNESCO as a World Heritage Site named the Golden Mountains of Altay. UNESCO states that "the region represents the most complete sequence of altitudinal vegetation zones in central Siberia, from steppe, forest-steppe, mixed forest, sub alpine vegetation to alpine vegetation". The mountain of Altay is a home to endangered mammals, such as the snow leopard and the Altay argali. Read more about Altai on the Russian information resource sites listed below:

- **www.waytorussia.net** - Type in *Altai, Siberia* in a search window.
- **www.raftsiberia.com** - Rocklin, CA.
- **www.geographicbureau.com** - A Russian based tour company, St. Petersburg.
- **www.altaimir.org** This WA based NGO provides lots of information about Altai.

Mount Elbrus, at 18,510 feet is the highest peak of Europe. It is located in southern Russia in the Caucasian mountain chain, which forms a steep spine connecting the Caspian and the Black Sea. Elbrus's permanent icecap feeds 22 glaciers, which in turn give rise to three rivers. Elbrus is an ancient volcano, although it has not erupted for nearly 2000 years. The first European to reach the summit in 1868 was an Englishman, Duglas Freshfield. Now Elbrus is a well known destination for climbers, mountaineers and hikers.

There are websites that hold a wealth of information about Elbrus and the Caucuses. You can find numerous articles on the history, geography, flora, and fauna of the region. An independent traveler planning a visit to the area would also find information on accommodations and transportation.

Here are some of the American and Russian companies that offer trips to Elbrus:

Pilgrim Tours (**www.pilgrim-tours.com)** sponsors an information website about Elbrus **www.elbrus.org.**

Mountain Madness, a Seattle-based company, specializes in mounting climbing, trekking and skiing all over the world. Check their website at **www.mountainmadness.com.**

Rainier Mountaineering, Inc. is another American company in Ashford, WA. that offers trips to Elbrus. Read more on these trips at **www.rmiguides.com** in the International section.

Additional information on Elbrus can be found at the following websites: **www.ewpnet.com** and **www.geographicbureau.com.**

The National republic of **Karelia** stretches for almost 372.8 miles to the north of St. Petersburg. Its capital Petrozavodsk was founded by Peter the Great in 1703. It is situated in the Russian lake district of more than 60,000 lakes of different sizes. Lake Ladoga and Lake Onega are the two largest lakes in Europe. Hundreds of rivers connect most of these lakes providing miles and miles of rafting opportunities. Kiji Island and Valaam Island with a monastery that dates back to 1329 attract many tourists. When a cruise-ship approaches Kiji Island, you see the first glimpses of wooden churches and log structures that were built without a single nail. It is an unforgettable and breathtaking sight you will cherish for many years to come. It is a magical place. Like Lake Baikal and the Altai Region, Kiji is a UNESCO World Heritage Site. To read more about Karelia go to **www.wikipedia.com**.

Intourist (**www.intourist.onego.ru**) is the best known tour agency in Petrozavodsk. Three other companies that offer trips to Karelia are:

- **www.nordictravel.ru** in Petrazovodsk, Karelia.
- **www.geographicbureau.com** in St. Petersburg.
- **www.mir-travel.com** in St. Petersburg.

CHAPTER 9

Restaurants to Discover: Casual and Fine Dining

Experiencing local food is as much a cultural experience as visiting museums, theatres, and monuments. Tasting local foods while traveling should be a part of your adventure.

In this chapter we will talk about several websites that list restaurants in Moscow and St. Petersburg by cuisine, location, and price. We will share our information on some of the best restaurants that we and our friends enjoyed immensely. Our list includes both affordable and upscale restaurants.

Here is the list of websites:

- **www.moscowcity.com** - Provides restaurant listings by cuisine, location and the nearest Metro station.
- **www.lonelyplanet.com** - Provides insiders' description of restaurants ambiance as well as their specialties.
- **www.saint-petersburg.com** - Provides restaurant listings by cuisine, location and the nearest Metro station.
- **www.fodors.com** - Provides the restaurants rating system.
- **www.globalhotelalliance.com** - Provides restaurant reviews (select your destination, then click on "*Restaurants*").

There are several Russian fast-food chains in Moscow and St. Petersburg. In fact, the term **fast food** can hardly be applied to these hearty homemade dishes served buffet style. Restaurants usually offer a vast variety of delicious appetizers, fresh salads, tantalizing entrees, and scrumptious deserts.

MOSCOW

Kroshka-Kartoshka or *One little potato* is a fast growing chain of restaurants with 140 outlets in Moscow and St. Petersburg. You can also find this chain in other Russian cities. Their signature dish is a baked potato with all kinds of fillings. Besides baked potatoes, the restaurant offers a variety of soups, salads, and traditional Russian dumplings filled with cottage cheese and different types of fruit. Some outlets are just food kiosks, while others are small and cozy restaurants. Meals start at $6.00.

Teremok is the name of yet another fast food chain. The name comes from a fairy tale and means a small house, or a little hideaway in the woods, where fairy animals find shelter. Their signature dishes are pancakes and hot cereals, such as cream of wheat, buckwheat, etc. You will find pancakes for every taste. Buckwheat is a popular choice in America only in the kosher isle, while in Russia it's an all-time favorite. Russian kasha is a meal in itself. The cereals are cooked with mushrooms, nuts, fresh and dry fruit, pumpkin, potatoes, beans, and bacon. Take for instance Gurievskaya cereal, cream of wheat with walnuts, raisins and dry fruit, served hot at *The Teremok Hideaway*. There are over 100 outlets in Moscow and St. Petersburg and their number is rapidly growing. Some are bright street kiosks, while others are restaurants. The company has a great website but unfortunately they do not offer an English version. The website in Russian is accessible at **www.teremok.ru.** In the restaurants meals start at $7.00, at the kiosks they start at $4.00.

The Russian Bistro, the first Russian fast food chain, opened in 1995 as an alternative to the then popular MacDonald's. This restaurant chain is famous for its pies. While in Russia, why not try little pies? The pies are stuffed with minced meat, poultry, cheese, mushrooms, fruit, and vegetables. The Russian Bistro also offers traditional dumplings (pelmeni), cold soup made with kvass, a traditional drink made of fermented yeast, (okroshka) and many other dishes. Meals start at $5.00.

The Russian chain of **Rostic's** restaurants recently signed an agreement with Yum, a corporation that owns KFC. It is a large chain of 300 restaurants and by the end of 2007 the chain had integrated popular Russian dishes into the most favorite KFC menu. Besides the original KFC recipes, the menu will include chicken shish kebabs, pies, and dumplings. Meals start at $8.00.

The name of another Russian restaurant chain **Elki-Palki** is a Russian euphemism somewhat similar to English expressions *Holy Smoke/Holy Moly*. The trademark of the restaurant is its cold buffet presentation on an immense ornate Russian wooden cart. Different vinegar-free pickled vegetables treated with salt and spices accompany over 30 different salads. It offers hot buckwheat, steamed cabbage, and hot potatoes as well. The buffet costs $9.00. Some of the outlets offer hot meal buffets. You can choose the salad bar or order a la carte. The menu offers traditional Russian food including pancakes with different stuffing, smoked salmon and sturgeon appetizers, wild mushroom soup, borsch, pelmeni, beef stroganoff, shish kebab and many other dishes. Elki-Palki offers a great variety of traditional Russian deserts. You should expect to pay between $15.00 and $20.00 for lunch or supper.

Moo-Moo is a small chain of 6 very popular restaurants in Moscow. It offers traditional Russian food and a large variety of international salads. The cost of salads varies from $ 0.70 to $ 2.00, entrees cost from $ 3.00 to $ 5.00. It is a cafeteria-style restaurant with hearty homemade food.

Drova means 'firewood' in Russian. The dining rooms in these restaurants are decorated with beautiful wood panels. It is an environmentally friendly operation. At present, the chain counts seven outlets in Moscow. A hot dish averages $12.00. The menu is eclectic: Japanese sushi rolls, Italian salads, Chinese appetizers, Russian soups, and French desserts. Recently the chain added a Japanese buffet at $22.00.

Japanese cuisine has become the latest fad. Several chains of sushi shops have opened their doors. You can't walk for 10 minutes without coming across a Japanese restaurant in downtown Moscow these days. The most popular is **Sushi Planet** with 19 outlets in the capital and other Russian cities. **Yakitoria** is another one where the menu counts 150 dishes. Another group of restaurants is called **Sushi Vesla.** The fourth popular chain is called **Tanuki** and is the most affordable of them all. Japanese restaurants are usually on the expensive side; the price of a meal can vary from $20.00 to $40.00.

Moka-Locca, Coffee House and **Shokoladnitsa** are coffeehouse style cafes. They offer a variety of coffees, snacks, sandwiches, and salads. These cafes in Russia offer more food choices than Starbucks or other coffee houses in the U.S. Some of them may offer business lunches. A cup of coffee may be priced at $4.00.

A more upscale restaurant where lunch starts at $20.00 and dinner at $30.00 is called **Sirnaya Dirka** (Hole in the Cheese). This small chain serves both French and Swiss cuisine. If you have a preference, be sure to ask for it. The menu offers dishes cooked with a variety of cheeses. Swiss cuisine is offered at the restaurant at 6/12 Pokrovksiy bulvar (Metro stations: Kitai Gorod, Turgenevskaya, Chistiye Prudi). French cuisine is offered at the restaurant on 32 4-9 Bolshaya Dmitrovka (Metro station: Tverskaya, Pushkinskaya, Chekhovskaya). Both restaurants are located in downtown Moscow.

If you like country style food, dine at **Korchma Taras Bulba** where a doorman dressed in traditional Ukranian costume greets you, then waiters and waitresses in folk dress usher you in to offer generous helpings of Russian and Ukrainian meat-and-potatoes dishes, beat-and-cabbage soups, and a vast variety of breads. There are six restaurants in this small chain and they are very popular among business people. Three are open from noon to midnight and the other three are open 24 hours. Here are their addresses:

Open from 12.00 p.m. to 12.00 a.m.

❋ 30/7 Petrovka street (Metro station Chekhovskaya, Grey line)

❋ 37 Leninskiy Prospect (Metro station Leninskiy Prospect, Orange line)

- 14 Piatnitskaya street (Metro station Novokuznetskaya, Green line)

Open 24 hours

- 13/14 Sadodovo-Samotechnaya Street (Metro station Tsvetnoy Bulvar, Grey line)
- 12 Smolenskiy Blvd (Metro station Smolenskaya, Light Blue line)
- 45, bld 2 Pokrovka Street (Metro stations: Krasniye Vorota or Chistie Prudy, Red line)

For fine dining we recommend two famous Moscow restaurants: **Pushkin** and **Turandot**. They are located next to each other in downtown Moscow, Metro Pushkinskaya (Purple line). Read a review on the Pushkin Restaurant in the New York Times online at **www.nytimes.com** (type in the name of the article "Where the High Rollers Dine"). See a write-up on Turandot at **www.passportmagazine.ru/article/432/**

There are some restaurants that offer an evening show to accompany a fine meal. **Godunov**, located across from the Bolshoi Theatre on Teatralnaya Square (Okhotniy Riad, Red line), is one of them. You will be entertained by dancing gypsies and traditional Russian folklore.

Another restaurant with evening entertainment is **Yar**. The restaurant is located at 32/2 Leningradskiy Prospect (Metro Dinamo, Green line). The restaurant offers Russian cuisine and a colorful show called "The Golden Domes of Moscow".

If you have a craving for good old American food, McDonald's, KFC, TGI Friday, Sbarro and Pitza Huts are everywhere in Moscow and St. Petersburg. There are three American Bar & Grill restaurants working around the clock. Their classic American atmosphere is enchanting. These restaurants' addresses are:

- 59 Zemlianoy Val (Metro Taganskaya, Brown line, Purple line; or Metro Marksistskaya, Yellow line).
- 1st Tverksya-Yamskaya Street (Metro Mayakovskaya, Green line)
- 50 Vorontsovskaya Street (Metro Krestianskaya Zastava, Green line); or Metro Proletarskaya, Purple line)

To read more on these and other restaurants, see restaurant reviews at **www.moscow-life.com**. Click on "*Eat*" and then on "*Restaurant Review*" in the top right corner.

ST. PETERSBURG

Most of St Petersburg's restaurants are casual, small, and cozy. Nevskiy Prospect, St. Petersburg's main street, is home to a variety of eateries offering different cuisines. Chain restaurants have not yet become a part of the restaurant scene. A list of St. Petersburg's restaurants by cuisine, location and Metro station is available at **www.st-petersburg.net.**

The following restaurants were found to be popular with locals.

Palkin was the first restaurant to open in St. Petersburg in the 19th century. Dostoevsky, Chekhov, and Chaikovskiy were frequent guests there. The restaurant offers Russian cuisine in a palacelike atmosphere, decorated with stunning chandeliers and impressive frescos. Gipsy shows provide entertainment on Tuesdays, Thursdays, Fridays and Saturdays. Address: 47 Nevskiy Prospect, Metro Mayakovskaya (Green and Red lines); or Metro Dostoevskaya (Yellow and Red Lines).

Dvorianskoye Gnezdo is situated in the Tea House of the luxurious Yusoupov Palace. Live music with violin, flute, and harp will accompany your dinner. This restaurant offers both Russian and European cuisine. Address: 21 Dekabristov Street, Metro Sadovaya (Blue line) and Metro Sennaya Square, (Yellow and Blue lines).

Chekhov dining rooms reproduce the atmosphere of a 19th century Russian mansion. The restaurant features Russian cuisine and you will enjoy piano music during your meal.

Address: 4 Petropavlovskaya Street, Metro Petrogradskaya (Blue line).

Russkaya Rybalka is located on a small pond where customers can catch their own dinner including trout, sturgeon, or starlet and choose how they want it cooked. A band plays at night. Address: 11 Yuzhnaya doroga, Krestoviy Ostrov, Metro Krestoviy Ostrov (Yellow line).

The Wave offers European and Italian cuisine with a breathtaking view of the Neva River and the summer residence of Peter the Great. The interior décor is black and white.

Address: 4 Petrovskaya Street, Metro Gorkovskaya (Blue line).

CHAPTER 10

Customs and Etiquette: To Kiss or Not to Kiss...

Non-verbal messages are coded on the subliminal level and, therefore, it is easy to misunderstand or misinterpret them if they are taken out of their cultural context.

In social settings, the handshake is a common form of greeting in the US. It is not exactly so in Europe. In tactile cultures, and Russia is definitely one of them, women greet people with at least two kisses on the cheek. Russians obey the law of the Trinity and kiss each other three times. Only men shake hands in informal situations. It is a taboo to shake hands without removing one's gloves. Women extend their hands and offer a surprisingly firm handshake but only in business settings. Passing objects, shaking hands, kissing, and hugging across the threshold is viewed as a bad omen. Touching each other in informal situations is acceptable in both cultures, however, a good-natured tap on the shoulder, or a friendly slap on the back, may be interpreted by the Russians as a condescending gesture.

Lounging in someone's living room with one's feet on the furniture is considered extremely rude even among friends.

A traditional Russian dinner is a sit-down meal. Vodka is usually served in tumblers and is consumed in one gulp. Leaving unfinished alcohol in your glass is considered rude. When dinner guests are present, a toast accompanies each round of drinks. Drinking without a toast is bad manners. Mixed drinks and cocktails are never served at dinner.

Russian hosts never offer a corner seat to a single or divorced guest. It is considered bad luck and the onset of seven years of solitude for that guest.

In Russia women often hold their women friends by the arm or lightly touch their elbows while talking to them, walk in the street arm in arm enjoying each other's company, none of which are signs that they are more than just good friends.

In Russia it is considered bad manners to point at people or each other, as well as objects with a finger. If an object has caught your interest and you absolutely want to point, use your whole hand instead.

Laws of North American hospitality do not encourage unannounced visits that are so popular in Russia. However, both in the US and in Russia, it is appreciated when guests bring a bottle of good wine and cut flowers. However, the difference lies in the number of flowers you bring; an even number is reserved only for funerals or cemetery visits.

Russians might think American tourists are obnoxious and loud. Americans might perceive an ordinary everyday conversation in Russian as a heated argument. When you witness two Russians engaged in a very peaceful and yet emotionally charged dialogue, do not jump to the conclusion that they are about to start a fistfight. Both Americans and Russians get wrong impressions and misinterpret intonations and body language. People tend to attach meaning to conversations based on how their own language flows or the gestures they use to convey an emotion.

North American questions "How are you?" "How is it going?", and even "How's life?" which some perceive as rhetorical greetings rather than actual enquiries, are not part of Russian culture where they are usually understood as invitations to a lengthy conversation.

In Russia as in many other countries you need to be observant and respectful of cultural differences. Enquire of your host or hostesses when you are in doubt.

CHAPTER 11

Memories are Free, Souvenirs are Not: Shopping Tips

As we travel to new places, we are always in search of the perfect memento to remind us of our adventures. There are thousands of trinkets, but finding something of quality requires knowledge and appreciation of the local culture. Here are some hints to help you find quality items that have the potential of becoming true memories.

It would be good to familiarize yourself with some of the best websites that cater to shoppers visiting Moscow and St. Petersburg and we will share some of our personal favorites with you.

There are valuable shopping suggestions at **www.lonelyplanet.com.** Type in *Moscow* or *St. Petersburg* and you will see the sections: see, sleep, shop, etc.

Another good website is **www.moscowcity.com/shopping** where stores are listed by category.

St. Petersburg has a municipal website where you can find information on everything from restaurants to shops. Go to **www.saint-petersburg.com.** Click on "*Shopping*" in the left column and you will see stores and boutiques that sell antiques, souvenirs, books, department stores, etc.

Another good website on St. Petersburg is **www.inyourpocket.com.** Choose St. Petersburg from a drop-down menu in the search window and click on "*Shopping*" on the horizontal bar.

Search engines like Yahoo or Google will bring up many hits if you put the following keywords in: shopping, Moscow, St. Petersburg. The shops will be displayed by neighborhood and by category.

MOSCOW

One of our favorite places to shop is Vernisazh, Moscow's crafts and flea market, where all traditional Russian crafts are represented. You can find matreshka dolls, lacquer boxes, samovars, beautiful feather light shawls, hand made scarves, tea and coffee sets, porcelain items, paintings, just to name a few. It is an antique lover's heaven because antique collecting is fairly new in Russia and you will surely find some treasures there. But you should know that if you buy something that is more than 100 years old, you would need a waiver from the Ministry of Culture to take it out of the country. Collecting Soviet-era memorabilia has become a new attraction for Russians as well as visitors. Don't be discouraged when vendors first quote you a high price. This is a place to bargain. There are hundreds and hundreds of stalls selling souvenirs. Vernisazh is a "must see". The market has so much to offer that it might become your sole source of souvenirs and it is an enjoyable place to wander around. Its facade is designed to resemble a Russian medieval fortress with its castles, guard towers, churches, and houses. The domes and peaks of the Vernisazh buildings are colorfully painted in bright blue, green, gold, and white. It is a picturesque, busy, and thriving market. It is open from 9.00 a.m. till 6.00 p.m. every day, but the best time to go is on weekends when all the vendors are there. The entrance fee is about $0.40 The market is located at Metro Partizanskaya (Dark Blue line). Once you exit the Metro, follow the crowd.

Read more on Vernisazh in the travel section of the New York Times at **http://travel.nytimes.com/2006/05/28/travel/28forage.html.**

Next to the Vernisazh crafts bazaar, there is another large open-air market where you can find quality clothing at affordable prices. Moscovites usually come in big crowds to shop on weekends.

Moskovskiy Department Store is another great place to shop for souvenirs. The store is open every day from 9.00 a.m. to 9.30 p.m. and is located on Komsomolskaya Ploszhad (Metro Komsomolskaya, Red line).

A few of our favorite souvenir places are located in downtown Moscow. The first one is Detskiy Mir (Children's World) on Loubyanskaya Ploszhad (Metro Loubianskaya, Red line). The Metro station is actually located in the same building as the store. It specializes in everything for children. You probably would not think of going to this big department store for souvenirs, but it is worth it.

Another souvenir shop is only five minutes away from Detskiy Mir on Kuznetskiy Most Street. Turn left on Kusnetskiy Most and you will see a large billboard advertising a popular vegetarian restaurant Jagannat. Next to it is a crafts and souvenir store. The store offers beautiful hand-made clothes, scarves, hats, pictures and paintings, as well as jewelry with gemstones from Russia and other parts of the world.

As you come out of the store, turn right, and keep walking straight to Petrovka, the next cross street where Kuznetskiy Most ends. You will see the four-storey Central Department Store (TSUM). It was the first department store that opened in Russia in 1857. The building has recently been modernized and now includes boutiques of major European designers. This is an upscale store and is certainly worth visiting.

Another popular and pricey Moscow department store is called the State Department Store (GUM). The facade takes up the entire eastern side of Red Square across from the Lenin Mausoleum. This three-storey arcade, with a fountain in the center, hosts many stores of European trading companies. The building is decorated with intricate wrought iron and a spectacular glass roof. You will find wonderful souvenirs made by the most distinguished Russian craft factories. However, high prices might persuade you to return to the Vernisazh where you can often find similar souvenirs at bargain prices. Read more about GUM on Wikipedia.com. Accessible from either of the two Metro stations: Okhotniy Ryad (Red line) and Ploszhad Revolitsii (Dark Blue line). GUM is definitely worth a visit.

Here are two very special Russian souvenir stores:

The Gus-Khrustalny Factory Store, a glass factory outlet featuring a wide selection of glassware, and Vologda Linen, a linen factory outlet. Both are located on Iliinka street in an arcade of small shops and business offices called Gostinniy Dvor. Gostinny Dvor is located across from St. Basil Cathedral. The nearest Metro station is Kitay Gorod (Orange or Purple Line), exit to Iliinka street.

To gather information for this book, we talked to our family and friends in St. Petersburg. They all agreed that a great way to shop would be to walk along Nevsky Prospect, the main street of the city, not forgetting to comb side streets where numerous privately owned boutiques may have better bargains.

A good place to shop is the chain of stores called ***OK***. Each of the ***OK*** outlets houses privately owned souvenir stands. ***OK*** outlets are located next to the following Metro stations: Ozerki (Blue line), Prospect Bolshevikov (Orange line), Ladozhskaya (Orange line), Prospect Prosveszheniye (Blue line).

If you are a porcelain lover, you should visit the Lomonosov Porcelain Factory outlet. One of the oldest factories in Europe, it was founded in 1744 by the daughter of Peter the Great. It used to belong to the Romanov family and supplied luxury tableware, porcelain dishes and figurines to the court. The factory continued its production through the revolution, and to this day it produces over 500 models of bone china dinner sets, tea and coffee sets, fine porcelain goblets, vases, and other pieces with conventional and new patterns. Read more about the factory at **www.rus-sell.com** (click on "*The Lomonosov Factory*"). The address of the Factory outlet store is 151 Prospect Obukhovskoy Oboroni, Metro Lomonosovskaya (Green line). If you didn't get a chance to go to the store in person, don't worry… You can buy your fine porcelain at **www.ekaterinas.com.**

A jewelry store *Samotsveti* features gems from the Ural Mountains and other parts of Siberia. It is located on Zina Portnova Street, Metro Leninskiy Prospect (Red line).

You probably know of the House of Faberge and a famous Russian jeweler recognized for his endless strings of decorative egg collections created for the Russian Imperial Family. If so, visit the Faberge factory store located at K. Faberge Square, Metro Ladozhskaya (Orange line).

Now that we have provided you with a list of stores and their locations, we would like to give you another tip. You will find regular department stores (*univermag* in Russian) at most Metro stations. And every one of them has a souvenir section or a counter. They are usually well stocked and prices are fixed with the locals in mind rather than the tourists.

Souvenirs convey the spirit of the places you visited. Buying souvenirs is a way of bringing the world into your home.

Our journey of writing this book has come to an end while the planning of your trip is just beginning.

Good Luck and Happy Travels!

Supplement 1

NORTH AMERICAN TRAVEL COMPANIES THAT OFFER TRIPS TO RUSSIA:

- *gotorussia.com*
- *expresstorussia.com*
- *mircorp.com*
- *russiantravel.com*
- *russia-travel.com*
- *mmarttravel.com*
- *traveleastrussia.com*
- *east-west-tours.com*
- *visitrussia.com*
- *altaimir.com*
- *mountainmadness.com*
- *elbrus.org*
- *Travel333.com*
- *Russia-travel.com*
- *raftsiberia.com*
- *cinderellatravel.com*
- *wnights.com*
- *greatcanadiantravel.com*

RUSSIAN TRAVEL COMPANIES CATERING TO FOREIGN TOURISTS:

- *travelinrussia.com*
- *waytorussia.net*
- *traveligit.com*
- *sv-agency.udm.ru*
- *reisebuero-welt.com*
- *moscow-hotels.net*
- *travel.org/firmata*
- *nordictravel.ru*
- *mosco.ru/eng*
- *123russia.com*
- *hostels.ru*
- *Russian-tours.spb.ru*
- *Welcome-to-russia.com*
- *baikaler.com*
- *baikalex.com*
- *travelkamchatka.com*
- *wildrussia.spb.ru*
- *kamchatkatravel.net*
- *kamchatkatracks.com*
- *kamchatkabear.com*
- *Baikal.ru*
- *irkutsk-baikal.com*
- *geographicbureau.com*
- *pilgrim-tours.com*
- *nordictravel.ru*
- *sochi2014.com*

- *Btgroup.ru*
- *Kamchatkapeninsula.com*
- *russia-ukraine-travel.com*
- *gotoru.com*
- *wild-russia.org*
- *spirit-of-moscow.com*

APARTMENTS TO RENT:

- *waytorussia.net*
- *aventec.ru*
- *kalitagrad.ru*
- *moscowapartments4u.com*
- *apartmentres.com*
- *flatlink.ru*
- *likehome.ru*
- *enjoymoscow.com*

AIR AND TRAIN TICKETS:

- *travelfleamarket.com*
- *expedia.com*
- *Travelocity.com*
- *orbitz.com*
- *kayak.com*
- *cheaptickets.com*
- *lowfare.com*
- *planetickets.com*

DOMESTIC TRANSPORTATION:

- *waytorussia.net*
- *visitrussia.com*
- *allrussiahotels.com*
- *gotorussia.com*
- *btgroup.ru (sochi)*

TECHNOLOGY FOR TRAVELERS:

- *gsmworld.com*
- *telestial.com*
- *mobal.com*
- *worldroam.com*
- *slowtrav.com*
- *intellicast.com*
- *vonage.com*
- *mywdt.com*
- *thetravelinsider.com*
- *cellularabroad.com*
- *smartcoms.com*
- *voltagevalet.com*
- *wtng.info*
- *skype.com*
- *voip.com*
- *startec.com*

MEDICAL HELP:

- *insuremytrip.com*
- *gateway2russia.com*
- *amcenters.com*
- *medem.ru*
- *russianadoption.org*
- *stpetersburg.usconsulate.gov*
- *emcmos.ru*

RUSSIAN MAGAZINES AND PERIODICALS IN ENGLISH:

- *russianlife.com*
- *passportmagazine.ru*
- *lenta.ru*
- *themoscowtimes.com*
- *Pravda.ru*
- *cigarclan.com*

RUSSIAN LANGUAGE COURSES IN RUSSIA:

- *derzhavin.com*
- *studyrussian.com*
- *studyrussian.spb.ru*
- *lidenz.ru*

STUDY RUSSIAN AT HOME:

- *rosettastone.com*
- *listentorussian.com*
- *byki.com*
- *russianlessons.net*
- *unforgettablelanguages.com*
- *guidetorussia.org (culture)*
- *russnet.org*
- *skypetutoring.com*

TRAVEL GUIDE BOOKS:

- *themoscowtimes.com/travel/whilehere/guides.html*
- *Berlitz Russian Travel Pack and Survival Russian from amazon.com*

FICTION BOOKS ABOUT RUSSIA:

Russka: The Novel of Russia by Edward Rutherford
The Madonnas of Leningrad by Debra Dean
The Amber Room by Steve Berry
The Romanov Prophecy by Steve Berry
Peter the Great by Robert K. Massie

Supplement 2

Hospitals and Medical Centers with Western Trained Physicians and Equipment in Moscow:

American Medical Center (accepts selected American medical insurance, you can become a member before the departure, 24-hour emergency assistance)

Tel: (495) 933-7700
Fax: (495) 933-7701
Website: **www.amcenter.ru**
Located at: 26/6 1st Grokholskiy Pereulok, Metro Sukharevskaya or Prospekt Mira

The American Clinic
Tel: (495) 937-5757
Fax: (495) 937-5774
Website: **www.en.americanclinic.ru**
Located at: 31 Grokholskiy Pereulok, Metro Prospekt Mira

Athens Medical Center/Hospital
The hospital has an intensive care unit.
Tel: (495) 143-2503 (emergency), (495) 143-2387, (495) 147-9322
Fax: (495) 147-9121
E-mail: 8112g23@g23.relcom.ru
Located at: 6 Michurinskiy Prospekt, Metro Universitet

European Medical Center (accepts selected American medical insurance, 24-hour emergency assistance)

Tel. (495) 933-6655
Fax (495) 933-6650

Website: **www.emcmos.ru**
E-mail info@emcmos.ru
Located at: 5 Spiridonievskiy Per., bldg. 1; Metro Pushkinskaya

International SOS Clinic (24-hour emergency assistance)
Tel: (495) 937-5760
Fax: (495) 937-5977
Website: **www.internationalsos.com/countries/russia**
E-mail: mow.marketing@internationalsos.com
Located at: 31 Grokholskiy Per. 10th floor; Metro Prospekt Mira

Italian Medical Center
Tel./Fax: (495) 234-9026
Website: **www.benessera.ru**
E-mail: cmi@zmail.ru
Located at: 28/1 Arbat Street; Metro Smolenskaya

Diplomatic Medincenter
Tel: (495) 237-3964
Fax: (495) 237-8475
Website: **www.medin.ru**
E-mail: medin@dataforce.ru
Located at: 4 Dobryninskaya Lane; Metro Dobryninaskaya

Russian American Family Medical Center
Tel: (494) 250-9186
Fax: (495) 932-8653
Website: **www.mediclub.ru**
E-mail: mediclub@cityline.ru
Located at: 10-2nd Tverskoy-Yamskoy Pereulok; Metro Mayakovskaya

DENTISTRY

American Dental Center
Tel: (495) 730-4334
Fax: (495) 730-3471
E-mail: info@americandental.ru
Website: **www.americandental.ru**

Located at: 5-1st Tverskaya-Yamskaya St.; Metro Mayakovskaya

American Medical Center
Tel: (495) 933-7700
Fax: (495) 933-7701
Website: **www.amcenter.ru**
Located at: 1 Grokholskiy Per. / 26/6 Prospekt Mira, Metro Sukharevskaya or Prospekt Mira

Adventist Health Center of Moscow
Tel: (495) 126-7906/ (495)126-7554
Fax: (495) 126-8767
E-mail: advhlthl@online.ru
Located at: 21a 60-Letiya Oktyabrya Prospect, Metro Akadamicheskaya

American Hospital in Moscow (24-hour assistance, you can become a member before the departure)
Tel: (495) 933-7700
Fax: (495) 933-7701
Website: **www.amcenters.com**
E-mail: amc.mrkt.co.ru
Located at: 1 Grokholsky Pereulok, Bldg 1, Metro Prospect Mira

American Russian Dental Center
Tel: (495) 797-9759
E-mail: americandental@co.ru
Located at: 21 a Sadovaya-Kudrinskaya St, 21a; Metro Barrikadnaya

European Dental Center
Tel. (495) 933-0002, night emergency: (495) 933-6655
Fax. (495) 241-81-08
Website: **www.emcmos.ru**
E-mail info@emcmos.ru
Located at: 6-1st Nikoloschepovsky Per., bldg. 1; Metro Smolenskaya

German Dental Care
Tel: (495) 737-4466
Website: **www.germandentalcenter.ru**

E-mail: info@germandentalcenter.ru
Located at: 2 Volochaevskaya St, Bldg 1; Metro Baumanskaya

Internatioanl SOS Medical Clinic
Tel: (495) 937-5760
Fax: (495) 937-5977
Located at: 31 Grokholskiy Pereulok; Metro Prospect Mira

U.S. Dental Care (accepts selected American medical insurance, you can become a member before you go)
Tel: (495) 933-8686
Website: **www.usdentalcare.com**
Located at: 7/2 Bolshaya Dmitrovka; Metro Okhotny Ryad & Teatralnaya

In the event of an emergency, you can contact the U.S. Embassy and check what assistance is available. During working hours call (495) 728-5577. After 6:00 p.m. call (495) 728-5000.

PHARMACIES (APTEKA)

American Medical Center Drug Store
Tel: (495) 933-7700
Fax: (495) 933-7701
Website: **www.amcenter.ru**
Located at: 1 Grokholskiy Per. / 26/6 Prospekt Mira, Metro Sukharevskaya or Prospekt Mira

International SOS Clinic Drugstore
Tel: (495) 937-5760
Fax: (495) 937-5977
Website: **www.internationalsos.com/countries/russia**
E-mail mow.marketing@internationalsos.com
31 Grokholskiy Pereulok, 10th floor; Metro Prospect Mira

There are two popular health and beauty retailers and Russian Pharmacy Chains called **36.6** and **Rigla**. Both provide excellent customer service and offer many American and European pharmaceuticals and over-the-counter medications, cosmetics, and facial care products. Many of the **Rigla** locations are opened 24 hours.

36.6

Numerous locations around Moscow.

Tel: (495) 797-6366

Web site: **www.pharmacychain366.ru**

E-mail: info@oao366.ru

Rigla

Numerous locations around Moscow.

Web site: **www.rigla.ru**

Tel.: (495) 730-2730

You can check medicine availability at Moscow drugstores by calling Medicine Information Service at (495) 927-0561

International Pharmacy Organization

If you can't find the medicine you need in Moscow, you can fax a copy of a valid prescription from your US physician or a Russian physician to the address below. Provide your credit card information and delivery address and your medication will be delivered to you within three working days.

85 Station Rd., Middlesex HA8 7JH, United Kingdom

Tel. 44 20 8381 1911

Fax 44 208 952 2063/44 208 951 4549/208 952 2995

Web site: www.theflyingpharmacy.com

E-mail ipo@aapi.co.uk , pharmacist@theflyingpharmacy.com help@theflyingpharmacy.com

OPTICIANS

European Medical center

Tel. (495) 933-6655

Fax (495) 933-6650

Web site **www.emcmos.ru**

E-mail info@emcmos.ru

5 Spiridonievskiy Per., bldg. 1; Metro Pushkinskaya

Lenmaster

Tel: (495) 928-4009/3473

Web site: **www.lensmaster.ru**

19/1 Nikolskaya Street; Metro Teatralnaya; plus many locations around Moscow

Ochkarik
Numerous locations around Moscow
Tel: (495) 231-1001
Web: **www.ochkarik.ru**

Interoptika
Tel: (495) 128-5717, 120-5200
Fax: (495) 120-8016
Web site: **www.english.interoptika.ru**
63 Nahimovskiy Prospekt; Metro Profsoyuznaya

MEDICAL EVACUATION FROM MOSCOW

Europe Assistance CIS
Tel: (495) 787-2178
Fax: (495) 787-2177
E-mail: info@europ-assistance.ru
Web: **www.europ-assistance.ru**
11/10 Letnikoskaya Street, build. 3, Metro Paveletskaya

Global Voyager Assistance
Tel: (495) 775-0999
Fax: (495) 775-0998
E-mail: info@gva.ru
Web: **www.gva.ru**
6 Prospekt Mira, Bldg 26; Sukharevskaya

International SOS 24 hour Alarm Center
Tel: (495) 937-6450 / 77
Fax: (495) 937-6472
Web site: **www.internationalsos.com/countries/russia**
E-mail: mow.marketing@internationalsos.com
16/1 Dokukuna Street, Metro Botanicheskiy Sad

Air Ambulance America
Tel: (1) (512) 479-8000 (call collect)
Fax: (1) (512) 472-8810
Web: **www.airambulance.com**

E-mail: aaa@airambulance.com
Austin Municipal Airport
P.O. Box 4051, Austin TX 78765

National Air Ambulance
Tel: 33335-1-800-327-3710 (toll free 24 hr.)
Tel: (1) (305) 949-6301 (Miami), (1) (305) 359-9900 (Ft. Lauderdale)
Fax: (1) (954) 359-9500
Web site: **www.nationalairambulance.com**
E-mail: inquiry@nationaljets.com
Ft. Lauderdale/Hollywood International Airport
P.O. Box 22460 Ft. Lauderdale, Fl

Air Ambulance Specialists, Inc.
24 Hour Dispatch Center
Tel: (720) 875-9182
Fax: (720) 875-9183
Web site: **www.AirAASI.com**
E-mail: info@AirAASI.com

AASI Corporate Office/Centennial Airport
8001 South Interport Blvd., Ste. 250
Englewood, CO 80112

American Care Air Ambulance
24 Hour Air-Evacuation Emergency Service
ICU, CCU, RN"s & Paramedics
ALS Medical Equipment on all flights
Tel: (858) 627-0515
Fax: (858) 627-0534
1 800-941-2582
Web site: **www.americancareairambulance.com**
E-mail: americancareair@aol.com
8775 Aero Dr., Suite #120
San Diego, CA 92123

Medical Services for International Visitors in St. Petersburg (with English speaking personnel).

EMERGENCY SERVICES/AMBULANCES:

American Medical Center	(812) 740-2090
Europed	(812) 327-0301
The International Clinic	(812) 336-3333
Coris Assistance	(812) 327-1313

American Medical Clinic
Tel.: (812) 740-2090 (24 hours)
Fax: (812) 310-4664
www.amclinic.com
78 Moika emb. 78, Metro Gostiniy Dvor

Euromed Clinic
Tel.: (812) 327-0301
Fax: (812) 327-0301
www.euromed.ru
Suvorovskiy Pr. 60; Metro Chernishevskaya

The International Clinic Medem
Tel.: (812) 336-3333
Fax: (812) 336-3334
www.medem.ru
Marata St. 6; Metro Mayakovskaya

Skandinavia
Tel.: (812) 336-7777
Fax: (812) 336-3060
www.avaclinic.ru
55-a Liteynyy Prospect; Metro Mayakovskaya

DENTISTRY:

American Medical Clinic
Tel.: (812) 740-2090 (24 hours)
Fax: (812) 310-4664
www.amclinic.ru
78 Moika emb., Metro Gostiniy Dvor,

Euromed Clinic
Tel.: (812) 327-0301
Fax: (812) 327-0301
www.euromed.ru
60, Suvorovskiy Prospect, Metro Ploszhad Vosstaniya 1 or 2

The International Clinic Medem
Tel.: (812) 336-3333
Fax: (812) 336-3334
www.medem.ru
Marata St. 6; Metro Mayakovskaya

Skandinavia
Tel.: (812) 336-7777
Fax: (812) 336-3060
www.avaclinic.ru
55-a Liteynyy Prospect, Metro Mayakovskaya

OPTICIANS.

Polyclinic # 80 – Eye Clinic (Trauma section is opened 24 hours)
Tel.: 272-5955 or 272-7834
25 Liteyniy Prospect, Metro Maykovskaya

PHARMACIES

American Medical Center
Tel. (812) 326-1730.
10 Serpukhovskaya Street; Metro Tekhnologicheskiy Institute

Petropharm pharmacy (opened 24 hours).
Tel.: (812) 314-5401 or nightline (812) 311-2077
22 Nevsky prospect, Metro Nevskiy Prospect

International Pharmacy Damian
Tel.: (812) 110-1744
22 Moskovsky Prospect, Metro Tekhnologicheskiy Institute

"Doktor" pharmacy (24 hours)
Tel.: 275-5634
7 Liteynyy Prospect, Metro Finliandskiy Vokzal

MEDICAL EVACUATION FROM ST PETERSBURG:

American Medical Clinic
Tel.: (812) 740-2090 (24 hours)
Fax: (812) 310-4664
www.amclinic.ru
78 Moika emb., Metro Gostiniy Dvor

Euromed Clinic
Tel.: (812) 327-0301
Fax: (812) 327-0301
www.euromed.ru
60 Suvorovskiy Prospect; Metro Mayakovskaya and Moscow station

The International Clinic Medem
Tel.: (812) 336-3333
Fax: (812) 336-3334
Web site: **www.medem.ru**
Marata St. 6; Metro Mayakovskaya

For American-based evacuation services see above list "Evacuation from Moscow".

www.ingramcontent.com/pod-product-compliance
Ingram Content Group UK Ltd.
Pitfield, Milton Keynes, MK11 3LW, UK
UKHW020138250726
13967UKWH00002B/735